fabulous cookies

fabulous cookies

SCRUMPTIOUS RECIPES FOR
DELICIOUS HOMEMADE TREATS

HILAIRE WALDEN

LORENZ BOOKS

First published in 2000 by Lorenz Books

LORENZ BOOKS are available for bulk purchase for sales promotion and for premium use. For details, write or call the sales director, Lorenz Books, 27 West 20th Street, New York, NY 10011; (800) 354-9657

© Anness Publishing Limited 2002

Lorenz Books is an imprint of Anness Publishing Inc.

Publisher: Joanna Lorenz
Project Editor: Joanne Rippin
Designer: Siân Keogh, Axis Design
Illustrator: Christos Chrysanthou, Axis Design
Cover Artwork: Balley Design Associates
Front cover: William Lingwood, Photographer; Helen Trent, Stylist; Sunil Vijayakar, Home Economist

Also published as part of a larger compendium, *The Great Big Cookie Book*

Printed and bound in Hong Kong/China
1 3 5 7 9 10 8 6 4 2

The recipes in this book were supplied by: Liz Trigg, Patricia Lousada, Carla Capalbo, Laura Washburn, Frances Cleary, Norma MacMillan, Christine France, Pamela Westland, Hilaire Walden, Elizabeth Wolf-Cohen, Janice Murfitt, Carole Handslip, Steven Wheeler, Katherine Richmond, Joanna Farrow, Judy Williams, Sue Maggs, Carole Clements, Jacqueline Clark, Sarah Maxwell, Sallie Morris, Lesley Mackley, Roz Denny, Sarah Gates, Norma Miller, Maxine Clark, Shirley Gill, Judy Jackson, Gilly Love, Janet Brinkworth, Ruby Le Bois, Elisabeth Lambert Ortiz, Sohelia Kimberley.
Photography by: Karl Adamson, Edward Allright, Steve Baxter, James Duncan, John Freeman, Michelle Garrett, Nelson Hargreaves, Amanda Heywood, David Jordan, Patrick McLeavey, Michael Michaels, Polly Wreford.

Recipe for Icing Glaze	Recipe for Royal Icing
1 tablespoon lightly beaten egg white	*1 egg white*
1 tablespoon lemon juice	*¼ teaspoon lemon juice*
3–4 ounces (¾–1 cup) confectioners' sugar	*8 ounces (2 cups) confectioners' sugar, sieved*
	½ teaspoon glycerin
Mix the egg white and lemon juice in a bowl. Gradually beat in the confectioners' sugar until the mixture is smooth and has the consistency of thin cream. The icing should coat the back of a spoon.	Mix the egg whites and lemon juice in a bowl. Gradually add the confectioners' sugar until the mixture reaches piping consistency. Stir in the glycerin until well blended.

Contents

Introduction

Americans call them "cookies" and the British traditionally use the term "biscuits", although now the word "cookie" has become quite common all over the world.

Whichever name is used, sweet cookies are delicious to nibble at any time of the day: with a cup of tea or coffee, or to serve with ice cream or other light dessert.

The American word "cookie" is of Dutch origin, from the word *koekje* meaning little cake. The origins of "biscuit" are to be found in the word itself: it comes from the French *bis cuit,* meaning twice cooked, and goes back to the days when bakers put slices of newly-baked bread back into the cooking oven, so that they dried out completely, becoming something like a rusk. This was really a method of preservation for it enabled the cookies to be kept for a long time; so long, in fact that they could be taken as a basic food item, known as "ship's biscuits", on long sea voyages.

For many years housewives continued with the practice of drying their biscuits a second time, and it was not until the beginning of the last century that the habit died out. Then both the quality and variety of biscuits improved dramatically.

A batch of homemade cookies will fill your kitchen with a wonderful aroma when they are ready to come out of the oven. There is a great difference between homemade cookies and the commercial ones sold in shops and supermarkets. Packaged, mass-produced cookies are more concerned with profit and long shelf-life. They are usually too sweet, contain additives and their character and flavor, let alone purity, cannot compare with a tasty cookie from your own pantry. Home baked cookies mean you can choose to use only the best ingredients.

There is almost no end to the range of cookies that can be made at home, using recipes that, over the years, have become great favorites the world over, with adults, teenagers and children alike.

This comprehensive collection of recipes suits every occasion and every taste, no matter if the fancy is for something rich and indulgent or traditionally wholesome, delightfully crisp or moist and chewy, satisfyingly chunky or elegantly thin, nutty or chocolatey. This book will inspire you to bake your favorite cookies for high days, holidays and special occasions, keep some dough in the freezer for unexpected guests, and determine never again to resort to the supermarket for your cookies.

▶ *Cookies are not only ideal for everyday eating, or special treats at home; they can also be gift-wrapped and given away as a special gift.*

Cookie Tips & Techniques

The Pantry

The ingredients for cookie making can be found in most people's pantries and refrigerators.

Chocolate Buy good quality chocolate with at least 50% cocoa solids for baking. Semisweet chocolate gives a distinctive strong, rich flavor while milk chocolate has a sweeter taste. White chocolate often does not contain any cocoa solids and lacks the flavor of true chocolate. It is the most difficult chocolate to melt and has poor setting qualities.

Eggs Eggs should be at room temperature so, if you keep them in the refrigerator, remove the number you want at least 30 minutes before making a recipe.

Dried fruits Today, most dried fruits are dried by artificial heat rather than by the sun, and are treated with sulphur dioxide to help their preservation. Oils are sometimes sprayed onto the fruit to give it a shiny appearance and to prevent it from sticking. Try to buy fruit that has been coated with vegetable oils, not mineral oils.

Butter and margarine Butter gives the best flavor to cookies and should be used whenever possible, especially when there is a high fat content, as in shortbread. However, it can be used interchangeably with hard margarine. Butter or margarine to be used for creaming with sugar needs to be at room temperature and softened. For rubbing in, it should be at a cool room temperature, not refrigerator hard, and chopped quite finely.

Soft margarine is really only suitable for making cookies by the all-in-one method and when the fat has to be melted.

Flours Flour provides the structure that makes the cookies. Always sift flour. Not only will this remove any lumps, which are rare nowadays, but it lightens the flour by incorporating air and makes it easier to mix in.

Self-rising flour has rising agents added and is the type of flour most usually used in straightforward cookies that need to rise.

All-purpose flour is used when rising is considered a fault, as when making shortbread. Rich or heavy mixtures that should be raised also often call for all-purpose flour plus additional rising agents in the specific proportions required for the particular recipe.

Wholewheat flour adds more flavor than white flour and is the healthier option but does produce denser cookies. When lightness is important extra rising agents should be added. Some recipes work well with a mixture of white and whole wheat flour.

Candied fruits Wash candied fruits before using them to remove the syrupy coating, then dry thoroughly.

Spices Ground cinnamon, ginger, apple pie or pumpkin pie spice, nutmeg and cloves may be used in cookies. All spices should be as fresh as possible. Buy in small quantities, and keep in a cool, dark, dry place.

Honey Honey adds its own distinctive flavor to cookies. It contains 17% water so you will need to use slightly more honey than sugar, and reduce the amounts of the other liquids used. Use honey within a few months of opening, and keep in a cool, dark, dry place.

Sugars Granulated sugar is the best sweetener to use for the creaming method because the crystals dissolve easily and quickly when creamed with the fat. Granulated sugar can also be used for rubbed-in mixtures and when the sugar is heated with the fat or liquid until it dissolves. Confectioners' sugar appears in the ingredients for some cookie recipes where it is important that the sugar dissolves very readily. Demerara sugar can be used when the sugar is dissolved over heat before being added to the dry ingredients. Soft light and dark brown sugars are used when a richer flavor and color are called for. Raw sugar is unrefined sugar which is uncolored and pure.

Nuts Nuts become rancid if stored for too long, in the light or at too high a temperature, so only buy in amounts that you will use within 1-2 months and keep them in an airtight container in a cool, dark cupboard. Alternatively, freeze them for up to 1 year.

Equipment

A delightful aspect of cookie making is that it requires a minimum of special equipment.

You can make a wide range of cookies with just a mixing bowl, measures or weights, a wooden spoon, a baking sheet and a wire rack. Only a few items are needed to extend the range much further. Many supermarkets now sell all you will need for cookie making.

Baking sheets Use good-quality sturdy sheets; thin, cheap sheets will buckle with time. Cheap sheets also heat more quickly so cookies are liable to cook quickly, brown and stick to them more readily. Nonstick sheets, of course, save greasing and lining when called for, greatly reduce sticking and cut down on washing up.

Cannelle knife This tool is great for carving stripes in the skin of citrus fruit. Pare off thin strips before slicing the fruit to make an attractive edge.

Cutters Cutters are available in many different shapes and sizes, ranging from simple plain cookie circles to small cutters for *petits fours* and savory cocktail nibbles, to animal shapes, hearts and flowers. For best results, the important criterion that applies to all cutters is that they should be sharp to give a good, clear, outline. This really means that they should be made from metal; plastic cutters tend to compress the cut edges.

To use a cutter, press down firmly on the cutter so that it cuts straight down right through the dough. Then lift up the cutter, without twisting it.

If you want to cut out a shape for which you do not have a cutter, the

thing to do is to make a template, or pattern. This is very easy.

Trace or draw the design onto waxed paper or cardboard and cut it out using scissors. Lay the template on the rolled-out cookie dough. Use the point of a large, sharp knife to carefully cut around the template, taking care not to drag it. With a thin metal spatula, transfer the shape to the prepared baking sheet, without distorting the shape.

Food processor Although food processors save time, their drawback is their very speed; they work so fast that you must be careful not to overmix a mixture. Food processors combine rather than beat ingredients together, so they are not so useful for recipes where lightness is important. Also, many models cannot beat egg whites, and even in those designed for beating, the whites will not become really stiff.

Knives A table knife can be used for the initial stages of cutting in the fat before it is rubbed in. Large, sharp knives are needed for cutting cleanly and efficiently through rolled-out dough or refrigerated dough. Metal spatulas are invaluable for spreading

and smoothing mixtures in cake pans, transferring cut-out cookies to baking sheets before baking and then transferring the baked cookies to a wire rack to cool. They can also be used for spreading icing on cookies.

Measures A set of accurate measuring spoons is vital for measuring 1 tablespoon, 1 teaspoon and fractions of teaspoons. All the amounts given in recipes are for level spoonfuls unless otherwise stated. For liquids, use a heatproof measuring cup, preferably see-through in 1-cup, 2-cup and 4-cup sizes.

Pastry brushes A large pastry brush is very useful for brushing surplus flour from work surfaces and cookie doughs that are being rolled out, and for greasing cake pans. A pastry brush is also needed for brushing on glazes. Buy good-quality brushes with firmly fixed bristles.

Piping bags and nozzles A medium icing bag with a selection of nozzles is very useful to have for piping uncooked cookie dough and for decorating cookies after baking. Use small disposable icing bags for chocolate or icing, where a fine line is required.

Rolling pin Rolling pins made of wood are the most common, but you can now buy marble or even plastic ones which are considered to be more hygienic.

Scales A good set of scales is essential for successful cookie making. Whether you use spring balance, modern electronic or old-fashioned balanced scales with a set of weights, test them frequently for accuracy by putting something on them which has the weight printed on it.

Sieves If possible have a set of strong sieves in 2 or 3 different sizes.

Skewers and toothpicks Either of these can be used for testing whether cookie mixtures are cooked.

Spatulas A flexible rubber spatula is indispensable for scraping every last morsel from the mixing bowl onto the baking sheet.

Swivel-blade peelers Both long-handled and broad-handled peelers are the best tools for peeling fruit.

Tea strainer A tea strainer will come in handy for sifting icing sugar over cookies as a last-minute decoration.

Whisk Use either a wire balloon whisk or a rotary whisk for beating eggs together. It is a good idea to have two sizes of balloon whisks, to suit the amount of mixture.

Zester Ideal for citrus fruit, a zester has the same function as a cannelle knife but produces a row of thin stripes.

Measuring ingredients

Cooks with years of experience may not need to measure ingredients, but if you are a beginner or are trying a new recipe for the first time, it is best to follow instructions carefully. Also, measuring ingredients precisely will ensure consistent results.

1 For liquids measured in cups or pints: use a glass or clear plastic measuring cup. Put it on a flat surface and pour in the liquid. Bend down and check that the liquid is level with the marking on the cup, as specified in the recipe.

2 For liquids measured in spoons: pour the liquid into the measuring spoon, to the brim, and then pour it into the mixing bowl. Do not hold the spoon over the bowl when measuring because some liquid may overflow.

3 For measuring dry ingredients in a spoon: fill the spoon, scooping up the ingredient. Level the surface to the rim of the spoon, using the straight edge of a knife.

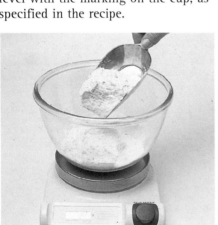

4 For measuring dry ingredients by weight: scoop or pour onto the scales, watching the dial or reading carefully. Balance scales give more accurate readings than spring scales.

5 For measuring syrups: grease the inside of a measuring cup before pouring in the required weight of syrup.

6 For measuring butter: cut with a sharp knife and weigh, or cut off the specified amount following the markings on the wrapping paper.

Making cookies by the rubbing in method

Plain cookies are usually made by rubbing the fat into the flour. For this, the fat, whether butter, margarine or lard, should be neither rock hard from the refrigerator, nor too warm. It is first chopped into small pieces, then added to the dry ingredients in a bowl. The mixture is lifted high and the lumps of fat rubbed between the fingertips as the mixture is allowed to fall back into the bowl.

1 Sift the flour into a bowl, adding the raising agents, salt and any sugar or spices and mix them evenly.

2 Stir in any other dry ingredients; combine the oats or other cereal, or coconut. Add the butter or margarine, cut into pieces.

3 Sprinkle the liquid ingredients (water, cream, milk, buttermilk or beaten egg) over the mixture.

4 Stir with a fork until the dry ingredients are thoroughly moistened and will come together in a ball of fairly soft dough in the center of the bowl.

5 Press the dough into a ball. If it is too dry to form a dough, add some extra water.

6 Turn the dough onto a lightly floured surface. Knead very lightly, folding and pressing, to mix evenly – about 30 seconds. Wrap the ball of dough in plastic wrap or waxed paper and chill it for at least 30 minutes.

Making cookies by the creaming method

To make cookies by the creaming method, the fat and sugar are "creamed" – or beaten – together before the eggs and dry ingredients are added. The fat (usually butter or margarine) should be soft enough to be beaten so, if necessary, remove it from the refrigerator and leave for at least 30 minutes. For best results, the eggs should be at room temperature.

1 Sift the flour with the salt, raising agent(s) and any other dry ingredients, such as spices or cocoa powder, into a bowl. Set aside.

2 Put the fat in a large, deep bowl and beat with an electric mixer at medium speed, or a wooden spoon, until the texture is soft and pliable.

3 Add the sugar to the creamed fat gradually. With the mixer at medium-high speed, or using the wooden spoon, beat it into the fat until the mixture is pale and very fluffy. The sugar should be completely incorporated.

5 Add the dry ingredients to the mixture. Beat at low speed just until smoothly combined, or fold in with a large metal spoon.

6 If the recipe calls for any liquid, add it in small portions alternately with portions of the dry ingredients.

7 If the recipe specifies, beat egg whites separately until frothy, add sugar and continue whisking until stiff peaks form. Fold into the mixture.

Making cookies by the all-in-one method

Some cookies are made by an easy all-in-one method where all the ingredients are combined in a bowl and beaten thoroughly. The mixture can also be made in a food processor, but take care not to over-process. A refinement on the all-in-one method is to separate the eggs and make the mixture with the yolks. The whites are whisked separately and then folded in. Soft margarine has to be used.

4 Add the eggs or egg yolks, one at a time, beating well after each addition. Scrape the bowl often so all the ingredients are evenly combined. If the mixture curdles, add 1 tbsp of the measured flour.

1 Sift the flour and any other dry ingredients such as salt, raising agents and spices, into a bowl.

2 Add the liquid ingredients, such as eggs, melted or soft fat, milk or fruit juices, and beat until smooth, with an electric mixer for speed. Pour into the prepared pans and bake as specified in the recipe.

8 Pour the mixture into a prepared cake pan and bake as specified.

Traditional Cookies

Granola Cookies

Makes 18

INGREDIENTS

½ cup butter or margarine
½ cup light brown sugar
⅓ cup crunchy peanut butter
1 egg
½ cup all-purpose flour
½ teaspoon baking powder
½ teaspoon ground cinnamon
pinch of salt
2 cups granola
⅓ cup raisins
½ cup walnuts, chopped

1 Preheat the oven to 350°F. Grease a baking sheet. Put the butter or margarine in a bowl.

2 With an electric mixer, cream the butter or margarine and sugar until light and fluffy. Beat in the peanut butter, then beat in the egg.

3 Sift the flour, baking powder, cinnamon and salt over the peanut butter mixture and stir to blend. Stir in the granola, raisins and walnuts. Taste the mixture to see if it needs more sugar, as granolas vary in sweetness.

4 Drop rounded tablespoonfuls of the batter onto the prepared baking sheet about 1 inch apart. Press gently with the back of a spoon to spread each mound into a circle.

5 Bake for about 15 minutes, until lightly colored. With a metal spatula, transfer to a wire rack and allow to cool.

Crunchy Oatmeal Cookies

Makes 14

INGREDIENTS

¾ cup butter or margarine
¾ cup sugar
1 egg yolk
1½ cups all-purpose flour
1 teaspoon baking soda
pinch of salt
½ cup rolled oats
½ cup crunchy
nugget cereal

Variation For Nutty Oatmeal Cookies, substitute an equal quantity of chopped walnuts or pecans for the cereal, and prepare as described.

1 With an electric mixer, cream the butter or margarine and sugar together until light and fluffy. Mix in the egg yolk.

2 Sift over the flour, baking soda and salt, then stir into the butter mixture. Add the oats and cereal and stir to blend. Chill for at least 20 minutes.

3 Preheat the oven to 375°F. Grease a baking sheet. Flour the bottom of a glass.

4 Roll the dough into balls. Place them on the prepared baking sheet and flatten with the bottom of the glass.

5 Bake for 10–12 minutes, until golden. With a metal spatula, transfer to a wire rack to cool completely.

Coconut Oat Cookies

Makes 18

INGREDIENTS

2 cups quick-cooking oats
1 cup shredded coconut
1 cup butter or margarine, at
*   room temperature*
½ cup granulated sugar
¼ cup firmly packed dark brown
*   sugar*
2 eggs
4 tablespoons milk
1½ teaspoons vanilla extract
1 cup all-purpose flour
½ teaspoon baking soda
pinch of salt
1 teaspoon ground cinnamon

1 Preheat the oven to 400°F. Lightly grease two baking sheets. Grease the bottom of a glass and dip in sugar.

2 Spread the oats and coconut on an ungreased baking sheet. Bake for 8–10 minutes, until golden brown, stirring occasionally.

3 With an electric mixer, cream the butter or margarine and both sugars until light and fluffy. Beat in the eggs, one at a time, then add the milk and vanilla extract. Sift over the dry ingredients and fold in. Stir in the oats and coconut.

4 Drop spoonfuls of the dough 1–2 inches apart on the baking sheets and flatten with the glass. Bake for 8–10 minutes. Transfer to a wire rack to cool.

Crunchy Jumbles

Makes 36

INGREDIENTS

½ cup butter or margarine, at
*   room temperature*
1 cup sugar
1 egg
1 teaspoon vanilla extract
1¼ cups all-purpose flour
½ teaspoon baking soda
pinch of salt
2 cups Rice Krispies
1 cup chocolate chips

Variation For even crunchier cookies, add ½ cup walnuts, coarsely chopped, with the cereal and chocolate chips.

1 Preheat the oven to 350°F. Lightly grease two baking sheets.

2 With an electric mixer, cream the butter or margarine and sugar until light and fluffy. Beat in the egg and vanilla. Sift over the flour, baking soda and salt and fold in.

3 Add the cereal and chocolate chips. Stir to mix thoroughly.

4 Drop spoonfuls of the dough 1–2 inches apart on the prepared sheets. Bake for 10–12 minutes, until golden. Transfer to a wire rack to cool.

Malted Oat Crisps

These cookies are very crisp and crunchy – ideal to serve with morning coffee.

Makes 18

INGREDIENTS

1½ cups rolled oats
¼ cup packed light brown sugar
1 egg
4 tablespoons sunflower oil
2 tablespoons malt extract

1 Preheat the oven to 375°F. Lightly grease two baking sheets. Mix the rolled oats and brown sugar in a bowl, breaking up any lumps in the sugar. Add the egg, sunflower oil and malt extract, mix well, then let soak for 15 minutes.

2 Using a teaspoon, place small mounds of the mixture well apart on the prepared baking sheets. Press the mounds into 3-inch rounds with the back of a dampened fork.

3 Bake for 10–15 minutes, until golden brown. Allow to cool for 1 minute, then remove with a metal spatula and cool on a wire rack.

Variation To give these crisp cookies a fruity taste, add ½ cup chopped dates.

Shortbread

Makes 8

INGREDIENTS

⅔ cup unsalted butter
½ cup sugar
1¼ cups all-purpose flour
½ cup rice flour
¼ teaspoon baking powder
pinch of salt

1 Preheat the oven to 325°F. Grease a shallow 8 inch cake tin.

2 With an electric mixer, cream the butter and sugar together until light and fluffy. Sift over the flours, baking powder and salt and mix well.

3 Press the dough neatly into the prepared tin, smoothing the surface with the back of a spoon. Prick all over with a fork, then score into eight equal wedges.

4 Bake for 40–45 minutes. Leave in the tin until cool enough to handle, then unmold and recut the wedges while still hot.

Oatmeal Wedges

Makes 8

INGREDIENTS

4 tablespoons butter
1½ tablespoons molasses
⅓ cup dark brown sugar
1¼ cups rolled oats
pinch of salt

Variation If wished, add 1 teaspoon ground ginger to the melted butter.

1 Preheat the oven to 350°F. Line an 8 inch shallow cake tin with waxed paper and grease the paper.

2 Place the butter, molasses and sugar in a saucepan over a low heat. Cook, stirring, until melted and combined.

3 Remove from the heat and add the oats and salt. Stir to blend.

4 Spoon into the prepared cake tin and smooth the surface. Bake for 20–25 minutes until golden brown. Leave in the tin until cool enough to handle, then unmold and cut into eight equal wedges while still hot.

Melting Moments

These cookies are very crisp and light – and they melt in your mouth.

Makes 16–20

INGREDIENTS

3 tablespoons butter or margarine
5 tablespoons lard or
vegetable shortening
½ cup sugar
½ egg, beaten
few drops of vanilla or
almond extract
1¼ cups self-rising flour
rolled oats for coating
4–5 candied cherries, quartered

1 Preheat the oven to 350°F. Grease two baking sheets. Cream together the butter or margarine, lard and sugar, then gradually beat in the egg and vanilla or almond extract.

2 Stir the flour into the beaten mixture, then roll into 16–20 small balls in your hands.

3 Spread the rolled oats on a sheet of waxed paper and toss the balls in them to coat evenly.

4 Place the balls, spaced slightly apart, on the prepared baking sheets, place a piece of cherry on top of each and bake for 15–20 minutes, until lightly browned. Allow the cookies to cool for a few minutes before transferring to a wire rack.

Chocolate Chip Hazelnut Cookies

Chocolate chip cookies, with a delicious nutty flavor.

Makes 36

❧

INGREDIENTS

1 cup all-purpose flour
1 teaspoon baking powder
pinch of salt
⅓ cup butter or margarine
1½ cups granulated sugar
⅓ cup light brown sugar
1 egg
1 teaspoon vanilla extract
⅔ cup chocolate chips
½ cup hazelnuts, chopped

❧

1 Preheat the oven to 350°F. Grease 2–3 baking sheets. Sift the flour, baking powder and salt into a small bowl. Set aside.

2 With an electric mixer, cream together the butter or margarine and the sugars. Beat in the egg and vanilla extract. Add the flour mixture and beat well with the mixer on low speed.

3 Stir in the chocolate chips and half of the hazelnuts, using a wooden spoon.

4 Drop teaspoonfuls of the mixture onto the prepared baking sheets, to form ¾ inch mounds. Space the cookies 1–2 inches apart.

5 Flatten each cookie lightly with a wet fork. Sprinkle the remaining hazelnuts on top of the cookies and press lightly into the surface.

6 Bake for 10–12 minutes until golden. Transfer the biscuits to a wire rack and leave to cool.

Chocolate Chip Oat Cookies

Makes 60

❦

INGREDIENTS

1 cup all-purpose flour
½ teaspoon baking soda
¼ teaspoon baking powder
pinch of salt
½ cup butter or margarine
½ cup granulated sugar
generous ½ cup firmly packed
light brown sugar
1 egg
½ teaspoon vanilla extract
¾ cup rolled oats
1 cup semisweet chocolate chips

❦

1 Preheat the oven to 350°F. Grease 3–4 baking sheets.

2 Sift the flour, baking soda, baking powder and salt into a mixing bowl. Set aside.

3 With an electric mixer, cream together the butter or margarine and the sugars. Add the egg and vanilla extract and beat until light and fluffy.

4 Add the flour mixture and beat on low speed until thoroughly blended. Stir in the rolled oats and chocolate chips. The dough should be crumbly. Drop heaped teaspoonfuls on to the prepared baking sheets, spacing the dough about 1 inch apart.

5 Bake for about 15 minutes, until just firm around the edge but still soft to the touch in the center. With a slotted spatula, transfer the cookies to a wire rack and allow to cool.

Mexican Almond Cookies

Light and crisp, these cookies are perfect with a cup of strong coffee.

Makes 24

INGREDIENTS

1 cup all-purpose flour
1⅓ cups confectioners' sugar
pinch of salt
½ cup almonds, finely chopped
½ teaspoon vanilla extract
½ cup unsalted butter
confectioners' sugar for dusting

Variation Try using other nuts such as walnuts, peanuts or pecans.

3 Roll out the dough on a lightly floured surface until it is ⅛ inch thick. Using a round cutter, stamp out into about 24 cookies, re-rolling the trimmings as necessary.

4 Transfer the cookies to nonstick baking sheets and bake for 30 minutes, until browned. Transfer to wire racks to cool, then dust thickly with confectioners' sugar.

1 Preheat the oven to 350°F. Sift the flour, confectioners' sugar and salt into a bowl. Add the almonds and vanilla extract and mix well.

2 Using your fingertips, work the butter into the mixture to make a dough. Form it into a ball.

Peanut Butter Cookies

For extra crunch, add ¹/₂ cup chopped peanuts with the peanut butter.

Makes 24

❦

INGREDIENTS

1 cup all-purpose flour
¹/₂ teaspoon baking soda
pinch of salt
¹/₂ cup butter
*³/₄ cup firmly packed light brown
sugar*
1 egg
1 teaspoon vanilla extract
1 cup crunchy peanut butter

❦

1 Sift together the flour, baking soda and salt and set aside.

2 With an electric mixer, cream together the butter and sugar until light and fluffy.

3 In another bowl, mix the egg and vanilla extract, then gradually beat into the butter mixture.

4 Stir in the peanut butter and blend thoroughly. Stir in the dry ingredients. Chill for at least 30 minutes, until firm.

5 Preheat the oven to 350°F. Grease two baking sheets.

6 Spoon out rounded teaspoonfuls of the dough and roll into balls.

7 Place the balls on the prepared baking sheets and press flat with a fork into circles about 2½ inches in diameter, making a criss-cross pattern. Bake for 12–15 minutes, until lightly colored. Transfer to a wire rack to cool.

Tollhouse Cookies

Makes 24

❦

INGREDIENTS

¹/₂ cup butter or margarine
¹/₄ cup granulated sugar
*¹/₂ cup firmly packed dark brown
sugar*
1 egg
¹/₂ teaspoon vanilla extract
1¹/₈ cups all-purpose flour
¹/₂ teaspoon baking soda
pinch of salt
1 cup chocolate chips
¹/₂ cup walnuts, chopped

❦

1 Preheat the oven to 350°F. Grease two baking sheets.

2 With an electric mixer, cream together the butter or margarine and the two sugars until the mixture is light and fluffy.

3 In another bowl, mix the egg and vanilla extract, then gradually beat into the butter mixture. Sift over the flour, baking soda and salt. Stir to blend.

4 Add the chocolate chips and walnuts, and mix to combine thoroughly.

5 Place heaping teaspoonfuls of the dough 2 inches apart on the prepared baking sheets. Bake for 10–15 minutes, until lightly colored. With a metal spatula, transfer to a wire rack to cool.

Snickerdoodles

Makes 30

❦

INGREDIENTS

½ cup butter
1½ cups sugar
1 teaspoon vanilla extract
2 eggs
¼ cup milk
3½ cups all-purpose flour
1 teaspoon baking soda
½ cup walnuts or pecans, finely chopped
For the coating
5 tablespoons sugar
2 tablespoons ground cinnamon

❦

1 With an electric mixer, beat the butter until light and creamy. Add the sugar and vanilla extract and continue until fluffy. Beat in the eggs, then the milk.

2 Sift the flour and baking soda over the butter mixture and stir to blend. Stir in the nuts. Refrigerate for 15 minutes. Preheat the oven to 375°F. Grease two baking sheets.

3 To make the coating, mix the sugar and cinnamon. Roll tablespoonfuls of the dough into walnut-size balls. Roll the balls in the sugar mixture. You may need to work in batches.

4 Place the balls 2 inches apart on the prepared baking sheets and flatten slightly. Bake for about 10 minutes, until golden. Transfer to a wire rack to cool.

Chewy Chocolate Cookies

Makes 18

❦

INGREDIENTS

4 egg whites
2½ cups confectioners' sugar
1 cup cocoa powder
2 tablespoons all-purpose flour
1 teaspoon instant coffee powder
1 tablespoon water
1 cup walnuts, finely chopped

❦

1 Preheat the oven to 350°F. Line two baking sheets with waxed paper and then grease the paper well.

2 With an electric mixer, beat the egg whites until frothy.

3 Sift the sugar, cocoa, flour and coffee into the whites. Add the water and continue beating on low speed to blend, then on high for a few minutes, until the mixture thickens. With a rubber spatula, fold in the walnuts.

4 Place generous spoonfuls of the mixture 1 inch apart on the prepared baking sheets. Bake for 12–15 minutes, until firm and cracked on top but soft on the inside. With a metal spatula, transfer to a wire rack to cool.

Variation Add ½ cup chocolate chips to the dough with the chopped walnuts.

Buttermilk Cookies

Makes 15

INGREDIENTS

*1½ cups all-purpose flour
pinch of salt
1 teaspoon baking powder
½ teaspoon baking soda
4 tablespoons cold butter or
margarine
¾ cup buttermilk*

1 Preheat the oven to 425°F. Grease a baking sheet.

2 Sift the dry ingredients into a bowl. Rub in the butter or margarine until the mixture resembles coarse crumbs.

3 Gradually pour in the buttermilk, stirring with a fork until the mixture forms a soft dough.

4 Roll out to about ½ inch thick. Stamp out 2-inch circles with a cookie cutter.

5 Place on the prepared baking sheet and bake for 12–15 minutes, until golden. Serve warm or at room temperature.

Shortcake Cookies

These make a simple accompaniment to meals, or a snack with fruit preserves.

Makes 8

INGREDIENTS

*1⅓ cups all-purpose flour
2 tablespoons sugar
1 tablespoon baking powder
pinch of salt
5 tablespoons cold butter, chopped
½ cup milk*

Variation For Berry Shortcake, split the cookies in half while still warm. Butter one half, top with lightly sugared fresh berries, such as strawberries, raspberries or blueberries, and sandwich with the other half. Serve with dollops of whipped cream.

1 Preheat the oven to 425°F. Grease a baking sheet. Sift the flour, sugar, baking powder and salt into a bowl.

2 Rub in the butter until the mixture resembles coarse crumbs. Pour in the milk and stir with a fork to form a soft dough.

3 Roll out the dough to about ¼ inch thick. Stamp out circles with a 2½-inch cookie cutter.

4 Place on the prepared baking sheet and bake for about 12 minutes, until golden. Serve these soft cookies hot or warm, spread with butter for meals. To accompany tea or coffee, serve with butter and jam or honey.

Traditional Sugar Cookies

Makes 36

INGREDIENTS

3 cups all-purpose flour
1 teaspoon baking soda
2 teaspoons baking powder
½ teaspoon grated nutmeg
½ cup butter or margarine
1 cup sugar
½ teaspoon vanilla extract
1 egg
½ cup milk
colored or raw sugar for
sprinkling

1 Sift the flour, baking soda, baking powder and nutmeg into a small bowl. Set aside.

2 With an electric mixer, cream together the butter or margarine, granulated sugar and vanilla extract until the mixture is light and fluffy. Add the egg and beat to mix well.

3 Add the flour mixture alternately with the milk to make a soft dough. Wrap in plastic wrap and chill for at least 30 minutes.

4 Preheat the oven to 350°F. Roll out the dough on a lightly floured surface to ⅛ inch thick. Cut into rounds or other shapes with floured cookie cutters.

5 Transfer to ungreased baking sheets. Sprinkle with colored or raw sugar. Bake for 10–12 minutes, until golden brown. Transfer the cookies to a wire rack to cool.

Brittany Butter Cookies

These little biscuits are similar to shortbread, but richer. Traditionally, they are made with lightly salted butter.

Makes 18–20

❧

INGREDIENTS

6 egg yolks, lightly beaten
1 tablespoon milk
2¼ cups all-purpose flour
¾ cup sugar
scant 1 cup butter

❧

1 Preheat the oven to 350°F. Butter a heavy baking sheet. Mix 1 tablespoon of the egg yolks with the milk to make a glaze.

2 Sift the flour into a bowl. Add the egg yolks, sugar and butter, and work them together until creamy.

3 Gradually bring in a little flour at a time until it forms a slightly sticky dough.

4 Using floured hands, pat out the dough to about ¼ inch thick and cut out rounds using a 3 inch cutter. Transfer the rounds to the prepared baking sheet, brush each with a little egg glaze, then, using the back of a knife, score with lines to create a lattice pattern.

5 Bake for about 12–15 minutes, until golden. Cool on the baking sheet on a wire rack for 15 minutes, then carefully remove the biscuits and leave to cool completely on the rack.

Cook's Tip To make a large Brittany Butter Cake, pat the dough with well-floured hands into a 9 inch loose-based cake pan or springform pan. Brush with egg glaze and score the lattice pattern on top. Bake for 45 minutes–1 hour, until firm to the touch and golden brown.

Toffee Cookies

Makes 36

❦

INGREDIENTS

¾ cup unsalted butter, melted
1¾ cups instant oatmeal
½ cup packed light brown sugar
½ cup dark corn syrup
2 tablespoons vanilla extract
large pinch of salt
¾ cup semisweet chocolate, grated
⅓ cup chopped walnuts

❦

1 Preheat the oven to 400°F. Grease a 15 x 10-inch baking pan.

2 Mix together the butter, oats, sugar, syrup, vanilla extract and salt and press into the prepared pan. Bake for about 15–18 minutes, until the mixture is brown and bubbly.

3 Remove from the oven and immediately sprinkle on the chocolate. Set aside for 10 minutes, then spread the chocolate over the base. Sprinkle on the nuts. Transfer to a wire rack to cool. Cut into squares.

Rose Water Thins

These light, crunchy cookies are easy to make and bake in minutes.

Makes 60

❦

INGREDIENTS

1 cup lightly salted butter
1 cup sugar, plus extra
for sprinkling
1 egg
1 tablespoon light cream
2½ cups all-purpose flour
pinch of salt
1 teaspoon baking powder
1 tablespoon rose water

❦

1 Preheat the oven to 375°F. Line two baking sheets with baking parchment.

2 Soften the butter and mix with all the other ingredients until you have a firm dough. Mold the mixture into an even roll and wrap in waxed paper. Chill until it is firm enough to slice very thinly. This will take 1–1½ hours.

3 Arrange the cookies on the prepared baking sheets with enough space for them to spread. Sprinkle with a little sugar and bake for about 10 minutes, until they are just turning brown at the edges.

Old-fashioned Ginger Cookies

Makes 60

❦

INGREDIENTS

2½ cups all-purpose flour
1 teaspoon baking soda
1½ teaspoons ground ginger
¼ teaspoon ground cinnamon
¼ teaspoon ground cloves
½ cup butter or margarine
1½ cups sugar
1 egg, beaten
4 tablespoons black molasses
1 teaspoon fresh lemon juice

❦

1 Preheat the oven to 325°F. Grease 3–4 baking trays.

2 Sift the flour, baking soda and spices into a small bowl. Set aside.

3 With an electric mixer, cream together the butter or margarine and two-thirds of the sugar.

4 Stir in the egg, molasses and lemon juice. Add the flour mixture and mix in thoroughly with a wooden spoon to make a soft dough.

5 Shape the dough into ¾ inch balls. Roll the balls in the remaining sugar and place them about 2 inches apart on the prepared baking trays.

6 Bake for about 12 minutes, until the biscuits are just firm to the touch. With a slotted spatula, transfer the biscuits to a wire rack and leave to cool.

Chunky Chocolate Drops

Do not allow these cookies to cool completely on the baking sheet or they will become too crisp and will break when you try to lift them.

Makes 18

INGREDIENTS

6 ounces semisweet chocolate, chopped
½ cup unsalted butter, chopped
2 eggs
½ cup granulated sugar
⅓ cup light brown sugar
⅓ cup all-purpose flour
¼ cup cocoa powder
1 teaspoon baking powder
2 teaspoons vanilla extract
pinch of salt
1 cup pecans, toasted and coarsely chopped
1 cup semisweet chocolate chips
4 ounces good-quality white chocolate, chopped into ¼-inch pieces
½ cup good-quality milk chocolate, chopped into ¼-inch pieces

1 Preheat the oven to 325°F. Grease two large baking sheets. In a medium saucepan over low heat, melt the semisweet chocolate and butter, stirring until smooth. Remove from the heat and set aside to cool slightly.

2 In a large mixing bowl, using an electric mixer, beat the eggs and sugars for 2–3 minutes, until pale and creamy. Gradually pour in the melted chocolate mixture, beating until well blended. Beat in the flour, cocoa powder, baking powder, vanilla extract and salt until just blended. Stir in the nuts, chocolate chips and white and milk chocolate pieces.

3 Drop heaping tablespoons of the mixture onto the prepared baking sheets 4 inches apart. Flatten each to 3-inch rounds. Bake for 8–10 minutes, until the tops are shiny and cracked and the edges look crisp; do not overbake or the cookies will become fragile.

4 Remove the baking sheets to a wire rack to cool for 2 minutes, then transfer cookies to the rack to cool.

Orange Shortbread Fingers

These are a real tea-time treat. The fingers will keep in an airtight container for up to 2 weeks.

Makes 18

INGREDIENTS

½ cup unsalted butter
4 tablespoons sugar, plus extra
for sprinkling
finely grated rind of 2 oranges
1½ cups all-purpose flour

1 Preheat the oven to 375°F. Grease a large baking sheet. Beat together the butter and sugar until soft and creamy. Beat in the orange rind.

2 Gradually add the flour and gently pull the dough together to form a soft ball. Roll out the dough on a lightly floured surface to about ½ inch thick. Cut into fingers, sprinkle over a little extra sugar and put on the baking sheet. Prick the fingers with a fork and bake for about 20 minutes, until the fingers are a light golden color.

Double Chocolate Cookies

Keep these luscious treats under lock and key unless you're feeling generous.

Makes 18–20

❧

INGREDIENTS

½ cup unsalted butter
⅔ cup firmly packed light
brown sugar
1 egg
1 teaspoon vanilla extract
1¼ cups self-rising flour
¾ cup rolled oats
4 ounces semisweet chocolate,
coarsely chopped
4 ounces white chocolate, coarsely
chopped

❧

Cook's Tip If you're short of time when making the cookies, substitute chocolate chips for the chopped chocolate. Chopped crystallized ginger would make a delicious addition as well.

1 Preheat the oven to 375°F. Lightly grease two baking sheets. Cream the butter with the sugar in a bowl until pale and fluffy. Add the egg and vanilla extract and beat well.

2 Sift the flour over the mixture and fold in lightly with a metal spoon, then add the oats and chopped semisweet and white chocolate and stir until evenly mixed.

3 Place small spoonfuls of the mixture in 18–20 rocky mounds on the prepared baking sheets, leaving space for spreading.

4 Bake for 15–20 minutes, until beginning to turn pale golden. Cool for 2–3 minutes on the baking sheets, then transfer to wire racks to cool completely.

Chocolate and Nut Refrigerator Cookies

The dough must be chilled thoroughly before it can be sliced and baked.

Makes 50

❧

INGREDIENTS

2 cups all-purpose flour
pinch of salt
2 ounces semisweet chocolate,
chopped
1 cup unsalted butter
1 cup sugar
2 eggs
1 teaspoon vanilla extract
1 cup walnuts, finely chopped

❧

Variation For two-tone cookies, melt only 1 ounce chocolate. Combine all the ingredients, except the chocolate, as above. Divide the dough in half. Add the chocolate to one half. Roll out the plain dough on to a flat sheet. Roll out the chocolate dough, place on top of the plain dough and roll up. Wrap, slice and bake as described.

1 In a small bowl, sift together the flour and salt. Set aside. Melt the chocolate in the top of a double boiler, or in a heatproof bowl set over a saucepan of hot water. Set aside.

2 With an electric mixer, cream the butter until soft. Add the sugar and continue beating until the mixture is light and fluffy.

3 Mix the eggs with the vanilla extract, then gradually stir into the butter mixture.

4 Stir in the chocolate, then the flour followed by the nuts.

5 Divide the dough into four parts, and roll each into 2 inch diameter logs. Wrap tightly in foil and chill or freeze until firm.

6 Preheat the oven to 375°F. Grease two baking sheets. Cut the dough into ¼ inch slices. Place on the prepared sheets and bake for about 10 minutes. Transfer to wire racks to cool.

Double Gingerbread Cookies

Packed in little bags or into a gingerbread box, these pretty cookies would make a lovely gift.

They are easy to make, but will have everyone wondering how you did it!

Makes 25

INGREDIENTS

For the golden gingerbread
mixture
1½ cups all-purpose flour
¼ teaspoon baking soda
pinch of salt
1 teaspoon ground cinnamon
⅓ cup unsalted butter, chopped
⅓ cup sugar
2 tablespoons maple or light
corn syrup
1 egg, beaten
For the chocolate gingerbread
mixture
1½ cups all-purpose flour
pinch of salt
2 teaspoons ground pumpkin
pie spice
½ teaspoon baking soda
4 tablespoons cocoa powder
⅓ cup unsalted butter, chopped
⅓ cup firmly packed light
brown sugar
1 egg, beaten

1 To make the golden gingerbread,
sift together the flour, baking
soda, salt and spices. Rub the butter
into the flour in a large bowl, until
the mixture resembles fine
breadcrumbs. Add the sugar, syrup
and egg yolk and mix to a firm
dough. Knead lightly. Wrap in plastic
wrap and chill for 30 minutes
before shaping.

2 To make the chocolate
gingerbread, sift together the
flour, salt, spice, baking soda and
Knead the butter into the flour in a
large bowl. Add the sugar and egg and
mix to a firm dough. Knead lightly.
Wrap in plastic wrap and chill for at
least 30 minutes.

3 Roll out half of the chocolate
dough on a floured surface to an
11 x 1½-inch rectangle, ½ inch thick.
Repeat with half the golden
gingerbread dough. Using a knife, cut
both lengths into seven long, thin
strips. Lay the strips together, side by
side, alternating the colors.

4 Roll out the remaining golden
gingerbread dough with your
hands into a long sausage, ¾-inch
wide and the length of the strips. Lay
the sausage of dough down the center
of the striped dough.

5 Carefully bring the striped dough
up around the sausage and press
it gently into position to enclose the
sausage completely. Roll the
remaining chocolate dough into a
thin rectangle measuring
approximately 11 x 5 inches.

6 Bring the chocolate dough up
around the striped dough, to
enclose it. Press gently into place.
Wrap and chill for 30 minutes.

7 Preheat the oven to 350°F. Grease
a large baking sheet. Cut the
gingerbread roll into thin slices and
place them, slightly apart, on the
prepared baking sheet.

8 Bake for about 12–15 minutes,
until just beginning to color
around the edges. Leave on the
baking sheet for 3 minutes and
transfer to a wire rack to cool
completely.

Spicy Pepper Cookies

Makes 48

INGREDIENTS

1¾ cups all-purpose flour
½ cup cornstarch
2 teaspoons baking powder
½ teaspoon ground cardamom
½ teaspoon ground cinnamon
½ teaspoon grated nutmeg
½ teaspoon ground ginger
½ teaspoon ground allspice
pinch of salt
½ teaspoon freshly ground black
pepper
1 cup butter or margarine
1⅓ cups light brown sugar
½ teaspoon vanilla extract
1 teaspoon finely grated
lemon rind
¼ cup whipping cream
¾ cup finely ground almonds
2 tablespoons confectioners' sugar

1 Preheat the oven to 350°F.

2 Sift the flour, cornstarch, baking powder, spices, salt and pepper into a bowl. Set aside.

3 With an electric mixer, cream the butter or margarine and brown sugar together until light and fluffy. Beat in the vanilla extract and grated lemon rind.

4 With the mixer on low speed, add the flour mixture alternately with the whipping cream, beginning and ending with flour. Stir in the ground almonds.

5 Shape the dough into ¾-inch balls. Place them on ungreased baking sheets, about 1 inch apart. Bake for 15–20 minutes, until golden brown underneath.

6 Allow to cool on the baking sheets for about 1 minute before transferring to a wire rack to cool completely. Before serving, sprinkle lightly with confectioners' sugar.

Aniseed Cookies

Makes 24

INGREDIENTS

1½ cups all-purpose flour
1 teaspoon baking powder
pinch of salt
½ cup unsalted butter
½ cup sugar
1 egg
1 teaspoon whole aniseed
1 tablespoon brandy
¼ cup sugar mixed with
½ teaspoon ground cinnamon
for sprinkling

1 Sift together the flour, baking powder and salt. Set aside.

2 Beat the butter with the sugar until soft and fluffy. Add the egg, aniseed and brandy and beat until incorporated. Fold in the dry ingredients until just blended to a dough. Chill for 30 minutes.

3 Preheat the oven to 350°F. Grease two baking sheets.

4 On a lightly floured surface, roll out the chilled dough to about ⅛ inch thick.

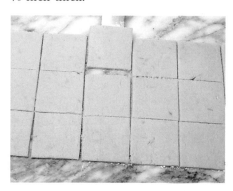

5 With a floured cutter, pastry wheel or knife, cut out the cookies into squares, diamonds or other shapes. The traditional shape for biscochitos is a fleur-de-lis but you might find this a bit too ambitious.

6 Place on the prepared baking sheets and sprinkle lightly with the cinnamon sugar.

7 Bake for about 10 minutes, until just barely golden. Cool on the baking sheet for 5 minutes before transferring to a wire rack to cool completely. The cookies can be kept in an airtight container for up to one week.

Festive and Fancy Cookies

Lavender Heart Cookies

In folklore, lavender has always been linked with love, as has food, so make some heart-shaped cookies and serve them on Valentine's Day or any other romantic anniversary.

Makes 16–18

◊

INGREDIENTS

½ cup unsalted butter
¼ cup granulated sugar
1½ cups all-purpose flour
2 tablespoons fresh lavender
florets or 1 tablespoon dried
culinary lavender, roughly
chopped
2 tablespoons superfine sugar for
sprinkling

◊

1 Cream together the butter and sugar until fluffy. Stir in the flour and lavender and bring the mixture together in a soft ball. Cover and chill for 15 minutes.

2 Preheat the oven to 400°F. Roll out the dough on a lightly floured surface and stamp out about 18 cookies using a 2 inch heart-shaped cutter. Place on a heavy baking sheet and bake for about 10 minutes, until golden.

3 Sprinkle with sugar then leave the cookies standing for 5 minutes to set. Using a metal spatula, transfer carefully from the baking sheet onto a wire rack to cool completely. The cookies can be stored in an airtight container for up to one week.

Vanilla Crescents

These attractively shaped cookies are sweet and delicate, ideal for an elegant afternoon tea.

Makes 36

❦

INGREDIENTS

1¼ cups unblanched almonds
1 cup all-purpose flour
pinch of salt
1 cup unsalted butter
½ cup granulated sugar
1 teaspoon vanilla extract
confectioners' sugar for dusting

❦

1 Grind the almonds with a few tablespoons of the flour in a food processor, blender or nut grinder.

2 Sift the remaining flour with the salt into a bowl. Set aside.

3 With an electric mixer, cream together the butter and sugar until light and fluffy.

4 Add the almonds, vanilla extract and the flour mixture. Stir to mix well. Gather the dough into a ball, wrap in waxed paper, and chill for at least 30 minutes.

5 Preheat the oven to 325°F. Lightly grease two baking sheets.

6 Break off walnut-size pieces of dough and roll into small cylinders about ½ inch in diameter. Bend into small crescents and place on the prepared baking sheets.

7 Bake for about 20 minutes, until dry but not brown. Transfer to a wire rack to cool only slightly. Set the rack over a baking sheet and dust with an even layer of confectioners' sugar. Allow to cool completely.

Fruit and Nut Lebkuchen

These simple, chunky gingerbread cookies make a delicious gift, especially when presented in a decorative gift box. The combination of walnuts, almonds and cherries is very effective, but you can use any other mixture of candied fruits and nuts.

Makes 20

INGREDIENTS

4 tablespoons granulated sugar
⅓ cup water
8 ounces semisweet chocolate, chopped
¾ cup walnut halves
⅓ cup candied cherries, chopped into small wedges
1 cup whole blanched almonds
For the Lebkuchen
½ cup unsalted butter
⅔ cup firmly packed light brown sugar
1 egg, beaten
⅓ cup molasses
3½ cups self-rising flour
1 teaspoon ground ginger
½ teaspoon ground cloves
¼ teaspoon cayenne pepper

Cook's Tip Carefully stack the cookies in a pretty box or tin, lined with tissue paper, or tie in cellophane bundles.

1 To make the Lebkuchen, cream together the butter and sugar until pale and fluffy. Beat in the egg and molasses. Sift the flour, ginger, cloves and cayenne pepper into the bowl. Using a wooden spoon, gradually mix the ingredients together to make a stiff paste. Turn onto a lightly floured work surface and knead lightly until smooth. Wrap and chill for 30 minutes.

2 Preheat the oven to 350°F. Grease two baking sheets. Shape the dough into a roll, 8 inches long. Chill for 30 minutes. Cut into 20 slices and space them on the baking sheets. Bake for 10 minutes. Leave on the baking sheets for 5 minutes and then transfer to a wire rack and set aside to cool.

3 Put the sugar and water in a small, heavy-bottomed saucepan. Heat gently until the sugar dissolves. Bring to a boil and boil for 1 minute, until slightly syrupy. Leave for 3 minutes, to cool slightly, and then stir in the chocolate until it has melted and made a smooth sauce.

4 Place the wire rack of cookies over a large tray or board. Spoon a little of the chocolate mixture over the cookies, spreading it to the edges with the back of the spoon.

5 Gently press a walnut half into the center of each cookie. Arrange pieces of candied cherry and almonds alternately around the nuts. Allow to set in a cool place.

Black-and-White Ginger Florentines

These florentines can be refrigerated in an airtight container for one week.

Makes 30

INGREDIENTS

½ cup heavy cream
¼ cup unsalted butter
½ cup sugar
2 tablespoons honey
1⅓ cups slivered almonds
⅓ cup all-purpose flour
½ teaspoon ground ginger
⅓ cup diced candied orange peel
½ cup diced crystallized ginger
7 ounces semisweet chocolate,
*   chopped*
5 ounces good-quality white
*   chocolate, chopped*

3 Drop teaspoons of the mixture onto the prepared baking sheets at least 3 inches apart. Spread each round as thinly as possible with the back of the spoon. (Dip the spoon in water to prevent sticking.)

6 In a small saucepan over a very low heat, melt the remaining chocolate, stirring frequently, until smooth. Cool slightly. In the top of a double boiler over a low heat, melt the white chocolate until smooth, stirring frequently. Remove the top of the double boiler from the bottom and cool for about 5 minutes, stirring occasionally until slightly thickened.

1 Preheat the oven to 350°F. Lightly grease two large baking sheets. In a medium saucepan over medium heat, stir the cream, butter, sugar and honey until the sugar dissolves. Bring the mixture to a boil, stirring constantly.

2 Remove from the heat and stir in the almonds, flour and ground ginger until well blended. Stir in the orange peel, crystallized ginger and ⅓ cup chopped semisweet chocolate.

4 Bake in batches for 8–10 minutes, until the edges are golden brown and the cookies are bubbling. Do not underbake or they will be sticky, but be careful not to overbake as they burn easily. If you wish, use a 3-inch cookie cutter to neaten the edges of the florentines while on the baking sheet.

5 Remove the baking sheet to the wire rack to cool for 10 minutes until firm. Using a metal spatula, carefully transfer the florentines to a wire rack to cool completely.

7 Using a small metal spatula, spread half the florentines with the semisweet chocolate on the flat side of each cookie, swirling to create a decorative surface, and place on a wire rack, chocolate side up. Spread the remaining florentines with the melted white chocolate and place on the rack, chocolate side up. Chill for 10–15 minutes to set completely.

Jeweled Christmas Trees

These cookies make an appealing gift. They look wonderful hung on a
Christmas tree or in front of a window to catch the light.

Makes 12

INGREDIENTS

1½ cups all-purpose flour
⅓ cup butter, chopped
3 tablespoons sugar
1 egg white
2 tablespoons orange juice
8 ounces colored fruit candies
colored ribbons, to decorate

1 Preheat the oven to 350°F. Line two baking sheets with baking parchment. Sift the flour into a mixing bowl.

2 Rub the butter into the flour until the mixture resembles fine bread crumbs. Stir in the sugar, egg white and enough orange juice to form a soft dough. Knead on a lightly floured surface until smooth.

3 Roll out thinly and stamp out as many shapes as possible, using a floured Christmas tree cutter. Transfer the shapes to the prepared baking sheets, spacing them well apart. Knead the trimmings together.

4 Using a ½-inch round cutter or the end of a large plain pastry nozzle, stamp out and remove six rounds from each tree shape. Cut each candy into three and place a piece in each hole. Make a small hole at the top of each tree to thread through the ribbon.

5 Bake for 15–20 minutes, until the cookies are slightly golden in color and the candies have melted and filled the holes. Cool on the baking sheets. Repeat until you have used up the remaining cookie dough and candies. Thread short lengths of ribbon through the holes so that the cookies can be hung up.

Christmas Cookies

Makes 30

INGREDIENTS

¾ cup unsalted butter
1¼ cups sugar
1 egg
1 egg yolk
1 teaspoon vanilla extract
grated rind of 1 lemon
pinch of salt
2½ cups all-purpose flour
For the decoration (optional)
colored icing and small candies
such as silver balls, colored sugar
crystals

1 With an electric mixer, cream the butter until soft. Add the sugar gradually and continue beating until light and fluffy.

2 Using a wooden spoon, slowly mix in the whole egg and the egg yolk. Add the vanilla extract, lemon rind and salt. Stir to mix well.

3 Sift the flour over the mixture and stir to blend. Gather the dough into a ball, wrap, and chill for 30 minutes.

4 Preheat the oven to 375°F. On a floured surface, roll out the dough until about ⅛ inch thick.

5 Stamp out shapes or rounds with floured cookie cutters.

6 Bake for about 8 minutes, until lightly colored. Transfer to a wire rack and allow to cool completely before decorating, if wished, with icing and candies.

Glazed Ginger Cookies

These also make good hanging cookies for decorating trees and garlands. For this, make a hole in each cookie with a skewer, when still warm, and thread with fine ribbon after it has cooked.

Makes about 20

❦

INGREDIENTS

1 recipe Golden Gingerbread mixture
2 recipes Icing Glaze
red and green food colorings
6 ounces white almond paste

❦

1 Preheat the oven to 350°F. Grease a large baking sheet. Roll out the gingerbread dough on a floured surface and, using a selection of floured cookie cutters, cut out a variety of shapes, such as trees, stars, crescents and bells. Transfer to the prepared baking sheet and bake for 8–10 minutes, until just beginning to color around the edges. Leave the cookies on the baking sheet for 3 minutes.

2 Transfer the cookies to a wire rack and allow to cool. Place the wire rack over a large tray or plate. Using a teaspoon, spoon the icing glaze over the cookies until they are completely covered. Set aside in a cool place to dry for several hours.

3 Knead red food coloring into half of the almond paste and green into the other half. Roll a thin length of each colored paste and then twist the two together into a rope.

4 Secure a rope of paste around a cookie, dampening the icing with a little water, if necessary, to hold it in place. Repeat on about half of the cookies. Dilute a little of each food coloring with water. Using a fine paintbrush, paint festive decorations over the plain cookies. Allow to dry and then wrap in tissue paper.

Easter Cookies

These are enjoyed as a traditional part of the Christian festival of Easter.

Makes 16–18

❦

INGREDIENTS

½ cup butter, chopped
⅓ cup sugar, plus extra
for sprinkling
1 egg, separated
1¾ cups all-purpose flour
½ teaspoon pumpkin pie spice
½ teaspoon ground cinnamon
scant ⅓ cup currants
1 tablespoon chopped candied
citrus peel
1–2 tablespoons milk

❦

3 Turn the dough onto a floured surface, knead lightly until just smooth, then roll out using a floured rolling pin, to about ¼ inch thick. Cut the dough into rounds using a 2-inch fluted cookie cutter. Transfer the rounds to the prepared baking sheets and bake for 10 minutes.

1 Preheat the oven to 400°F. Lightly grease two baking sheets. Beat together the butter and sugar, then beat in the egg yolk.

2 Sift the flour and spices over the egg mixture, then fold in with the currants and peel, adding sufficient milk to make a fairly soft dough.

4 Beat the egg white, then brush over the cookies. Sprinkle with sugar and return to the oven for another 10 minutes, until golden. Transfer to a wire rack to cool.

Golden Raisin Cornmeal Cookies

These little yellow cookies come from the Veneto region of Italy.

Makes 48

INGREDIENTS

½ cup golden raisins
1 cup finely ground yellow
cornmeal
1½ cups all-purpose flour
1½ teaspoons baking powder
pinch of salt
1 cup butter
1 cup sugar
2 eggs
1 tablespoon marsala or
1 teaspoon vanilla extract

1 Soak the golden raisins in a small bowl of warm water for 15 minutes. Drain. Preheat the oven to 350°F. Grease a baking sheet.

2 Sift the cornmeal, flour, baking powder and salt together into a mixing bowl. Set aside.

3 Cream the butter and sugar until light and fluffy. Beat in the eggs, one at a time. Beat in the marsala or vanilla extract.

4 Add the dry ingredients to the butter mixture, beating until well blended. Stir in the golden raisins.

5 Drop heaping teaspoons of the mixture onto the prepared baking sheet in rows about 2 inches apart. Bake for 7–8 minutes, until the cookies are golden brown at the edges. Transfer to a wire rack to cool.

Amaretti

Almond extract will provide the flavor of bitter almonds, which are not available in the U.S.

Makes 36

INGREDIENTS

1¾ cups almonds
flour for dusting
1 cup superfine sugar
2 egg whites
½ teaspoon almond extract or
1 teaspoon vanilla extract
confectioners' sugar for dusting

1 Preheat the oven to 325°F. Peel the almonds by dropping them into a saucepan of boiling water for 1–2 minutes. Drain. Rub the almonds in a cloth to remove the skins.

2 Place the almonds on a baking sheet and let them dry out in the oven for 10–15 minutes without browning. Remove from the oven and allow to cool. Turn the oven off. Dust the almonds with flour.

3 Grind the almonds with half of the sugar in a food processor. Use an electric beater or wire whisk to beat the egg whites until they form soft peaks.

4 Sprinkle over half the remaining sugar and continue beating until stiff peaks are formed. Gently fold in the remaining sugar, the almond or vanilla extract and the almonds.

5 Spoon the almond mixture into a pastry bag fitted with a smooth nozzle. Pipe out the mixture in rounds the size of a walnut. Sprinkle lightly with the confectioners' sugar, and let stand for 2 hours. Near the end of this time, turn the oven on again and preheat to 350°F.

6 Bake for 15 minutes, until pale gold. Remove from the oven and cool on a wire rack.

Decorated Chocolate Lebkuchen

Wrapped in paper or cellophane, or beautifully boxed, these decorated cookies make a lovely present. Don't make them too far in advance as the chocolate will gradually discolor.

Makes 40

❧

INGREDIENTS

1 recipe Lebkuchen mixture
4 ounces semisweet chocolate, chopped
4 ounces milk chocolate, chopped
4 ounces white chocolate, chopped
chocolate sprinkles, for sprinkling
cocoa powder or confectioners' sugar for dusting

❧

1 Grease two baking sheets. Roll out just over half of the Lebkuchen mixture until ¼ inch thick. Cut out heart shapes, using a 1¾-inch heart-shaped cutter. Transfer to the baking sheets. Gather the trimmings together with the remaining dough and cut into 20 pieces. Roll into balls and place on the baking sheet. Flatten each ball slightly with your fingers.

2 Chill both sheets for 30 minutes. Preheat the oven to 350°F. Bake for 8–10 minutes. Cool on a wire rack.

3 Melt the semisweet chocolate in a heatproof bowl over a small saucepan of hot water. Melt the milk and white chocolate in separate bowls.

4 Make three small paper pastry bags out of waxed paper. Spoon a little of each chocolate into the three paper pastry bags and reserve. Spoon a little semisweet chocolate over one third of the cookies, spreading it slightly to cover them completely. (Tapping the rack gently will help the chocolate to run down the sides.)

5 Snip the merest tip from the bag of white chocolate and drizzle it over some of the coated biscuits, to give a decorative finish.

6 Sprinkle the chocolate sprinkles over the semisweet chocolate-coated cookies that haven't been decorated. Coat the remaining cookies with the milk and white chocolate and decorate some of these with more chocolate from the piping bags, contrasting the colors. Scatter more undecorated cookies with chocolate sprinkles. Allow the cookies to set.

7 Transfer the undecorated cookies to a plate or tray and dust with cocoa powder or confectioners' sugar.

Cook's Tip If the chocolate in the bowls starts to set before you have finished decorating, put the bowls back over the heat for 1–2 minutes. If the chocolate in the pastry bags starts to harden, microwave briefly or put in a clean bowl over a pan of simmering water until soft.

Macaroons

Freshly ground almonds, lightly toasted beforehand to intensify the flavor,

give these macaroons their rich taste and texture so, for best results,

avoid using already-ground almonds as a shortcut.

Makes 12

INGREDIENTS

*1½ cups blanched almonds,
toasted
¾ cup granulated sugar
2 egg whites
½ teaspoon almond or vanilla
extract
confectioners' sugar for dusting*

1 Preheat the oven to 350°F. Line a large baking sheet with baking parchment. Reserve 12 almonds for decorating. In a food processor grind the rest of the almonds with the sugar.

2 With the machine running, slowly pour in enough of the egg whites to form a soft dough. Add the almond or vanilla extract and pulse to mix.

3 With moistened hands, shape the mixture into walnut-size balls and arrange on the baking sheet.

4 Press one of the reserved almonds onto each ball, flattening them slightly, and dust lightly with confectioners' sugar. Bake for about 10–12 minutes, until the tops are golden and feel slightly firm. Transfer to a wire rack, cool slightly, then peel the cookies off the paper and allow to cool completely.

Cook's Tip To toast the almonds, spread them on a baking sheet and bake in the preheated oven for 10–15 minutes, until golden. Allow to cool before grinding.

Madeleines

These little tea cakes, baked in a special pan with shell-shaped cups,

were made famous by Marcel Proust, whose great fiction starts off with

the taste of a madeleine.

Makes 12

INGREDIENTS

*1¼ cups all-purpose flour
1 teaspoon baking powder
2 eggs
¾ cup confectioners' sugar, plus
extra for dusting
grated rind of 1 lemon or orange
1 tablespoon lemon or orange
juice
6 tablespoons unsalted butter,
melted and slightly cooled*

1 Preheat the oven to 375°F. Generously butter a 12-cup madeleine pan. Sift together the flour and baking powder.

2 Using an electric mixer, beat the eggs and confectioners' sugar for 5–7 minutes, until thick and creamy and the mixture forms a ribbon when the beaters are lifted. Gently fold in the lemon or orange rind and juice.

3 Beginning with the flour mixture, alternately fold in the flour and melted butter in four batches. Allow the mixture to stand for 10 minutes, then carefully spoon into the pan. Tap gently to release any air bubbles.

4 Bake for 12–15 minutes, rotating the pan halfway through cooking, until a skewer or cake tester inserted in the center comes out clean. Turn onto a wire rack to cool and dust with confectioners' sugar before serving.

Cook's Tip If you don't have a special pan for making madeleines, you can use a muffin pan, preferably with a nonstick coating. The cakes won't have the characteristic ridges and shell shape, but they are quite pretty dusted with a little confectioners' sugar.

Tuiles d'Amandes

These cookies are named after the French roof tiles they so resemble. Making them can be difficult, so bake only four at a time until you get the knack. With a little practice you will find them easy.

Makes 24

୧

INGREDIENTS

generous ½ cup whole blanched almonds, lightly toasted
⅓ cup sugar
3 tablespoons unsalted butter
2 egg whites
½ teaspoon almond extract
scant ¼ cup all-purpose flour, sifted
½ cup slivered almonds

୧

Cook's Tip If the tuiles flatten or lose their crispness, reheat them on a baking sheet in a moderate oven until completely flat, then reshape.

1 Preheat the oven to 400°F. Generously butter two heavy baking sheets.

2 Place the almonds and about 2 tablespoons of the sugar in a food processor fitted with the metal blade and process until finely ground.

3 Beat the butter until creamy, then add the remaining sugar and beat until light and fluffy. Gradually beat in the egg whites, then add the almond extract. Sift the flour over the butter mixture, fold in, then fold in the ground almond mixture.

4 Drop tablespoonfuls of the mixture onto the prepared baking sheets about 6 inches apart. With the back of a wet spoon, spread each mound into a paper-thin 3 inch round. (Don't worry if holes appear, they will fill in.) Sprinkle with slivered almonds.

5 Bake the cookies, one sheet at a time, for 5–6 minutes, until the edges are golden and the centers still pale. Working quickly, use a thin spatula to loosen the edges of one cookie. Lift the cookie on the spatula and place over a rolling pin, then press down the sides of the cookie to curve it.

6 Continue shaping the cookies, transferring them to a wire rack as they cool. If they become too crisp to shape, return the baking sheet to the hot oven for 15–30 seconds, then continue as above.

Slivered Almond Cookies

Makes 30

🌿

INGREDIENTS

¾ cup butter or margarine,
chopped
2 cups self-rising flour
⅔ cup sugar
½ teaspoon ground cinnamon
1 egg, separated
2 tablespoons cold water
½ cup slivered almonds

🌿

3 Using a floured fluted round cutter, cut the dough into rounds. Use a metal spatula to lift them onto an ungreased baking sheet. Re-form the dough and cut more rounds to use all the dough. Beat the egg white lightly, brush it over the cookies, and sprinkle over the remaining sugar.

4 Bake for about 10–15 minutes, until golden. To remove, slide a metal spatula under the cookies, which will still seem a bit soft, but they harden as they cool. Let stand on a wire rack until quite cold.

1 Preheat the oven to 350°F. Rub the butter or margarine into the flour. Reserve 1 tablespoon of the sugar and mix the rest with the cinnamon. Stir into the flour and then add the egg yolk and cold water and mix to a firm dough.

2 Roll out the dough on a lightly floured board to ½ inch thick. Sprinkle over the almonds. Continue rolling until the dough is approximately ¼ inch thick.

Mocha Viennese Swirls

Makes 20

INGREDIENTS

*9 ounces semisweet chocolate,
chopped
scant 1 cup unsalted butter
½ cup confectioners' sugar
2 tablespoons strong black coffee
1¾ cups all-purpose flour
½ cup cornstarch
about 20 blanched almonds*

Cook's Tip If the mixture is too stiff
to pipe, soften it with a little more
black coffee.

1 Preheat the oven to 375°F.
Lightly grease two large baking
sheets. Melt 4 ounces of the chocolate
in a heatproof bowl over a saucepan
of hot water. Cream the butter with
the confectioners' sugar in a bowl
until smooth and pale. Beat in the
melted chocolate, then the strong
black coffee.

2 Sift the flour and cornstarch over
the mixture. Fold in lightly and
evenly to make a soft mixture.

3 Spoon the mixture into a piping
bag fitted with a large star nozzle
and pipe 20 swirls on the prepared
baking sheets, allowing room for
spreading during baking.

4 Press an almond into the center
of each swirl. Bake for about
15 minutes, until the cookies are firm
and just beginning to brown. Allow
to cool for about 10 minutes on the
baking sheets, then lift carefully on
to a wire rack to cool completely.

5 Melt the remaining chocolate and
dip the base of each swirl to coat.
Place on a sheet of baking parchment
and allow to set.

Chocolate Amaretti

Makes 24

INGREDIENTS

1¼ cups blanched whole almonds
scant ½ cup superfine sugar
1 tablespoon cocoa powder
2 tablespoons confectioners' sugar
2 egg whites
pinch of cream of tartar
1 teaspoon almond extract
slivered almonds, to decorate

1 Preheat the oven to 350°F. Place the blanched almonds on a baking sheet and bake for 10–12 minutes, until golden brown. Set aside to cool. Reduce the oven temperature to 325°F. Line a large baking sheet with baking parchment. In a food processor, process the almonds with half the superfine sugar until they are finely ground, but not oily. Transfer to a bowl and sift in the cocoa and confectioners' sugar. Set aside.

2 In a mixing bowl with an electric mixer, beat the egg whites and cream of tartar until stiff peaks form. Sprinkle in the remaining superfine sugar a tablespoon at a time, beating well after each addition, and continue beating until the whites are glossy and stiff. Beat in the almond extract.

3 Sprinkle over the almond-sugar mixture and gently fold into the beaten egg whites until just blended. Spoon the mixture into a large pastry bag fitted with a plain ½-inch nozzle. Pipe 1½-inch rounds about 1 inch apart on the prepared baking sheet. Press a slivered almond into the center of each.

4 Bake the cookies for 12–15 minutes, or until crisp. Remove the baking sheets to a wire rack to cool for 10 minutes. With a metal spatula, remove the amaretti to a wire rack to cool completely.

Nut Lace Cookies

Makes 18

INGREDIENTS

½ cup blanched almonds
4 tablespoons butter
3 tablespoons all-purpose flour
½ cup sugar
2 tablespoons heavy cream
½ teaspoon vanilla extract

Variation Add ¼ cup finely chopped candied orange peel to the mixture.

1 Preheat the oven to 375°F. Grease 1–2 baking sheets.

2 With a sharp knife, chop the almonds as finely as possible. Alternatively, use a food processor, blender or nut grinder to chop the nuts very finely.

3 Melt the butter in a small saucepan over low heat. Remove from the heat and stir in the remaining ingredients, including the almonds.

4 Drop teaspoonfuls of the mixture 2½ inches apart on the prepared baking sheets. Bake for about 5 minutes, until golden. Cool on the sheets briefly, until the cookies are just stiff enough to lift off.

5 With a metal spatula, transfer the cookies to a wire rack to cool completely.

Oatmeal Lace Cookies

Makes 36

INGREDIENTS

⅔ cup butter or margarine
1½ cups rolled oats
¾ cup firmly packed dark brown sugar
¾ cup granulated sugar
3 tablespoons all-purpose flour
pinch of salt
1 egg, lightly beaten
1 teaspoon vanilla extract
½ cup pecans or walnuts, finely chopped

1 Preheat the oven to 350°F. Grease two baking sheets.

2 Melt the butter or margarine in a small saucepan over low heat. Set aside.

3 In a mixing bowl, combine the oats, brown sugar, granulated sugar, flour and salt.

4 Add the butter or margarine, the egg and vanilla extract.

5 Mix until blended, then stir in the chopped nuts.

6 Drop rounded teaspoonfuls of the batter about 2 inches apart on the prepared baking sheets. Bake for 5–8 minutes, until lightly browned on the edges and bubbling. Allow to cool for 2 minutes, then transfer to a wire rack to cool completely.

Raspberry Sandwich Cookies

Children will love these sweet, sticky treats.

Makes 32

INGREDIENTS

1 cup blanched almonds
1½ cups all-purpose flour
¾ cup butter
½ cup sugar
grated rind of 1 lemon
1 teaspoon vanilla extract
1 egg white
pinch of salt
⅓ cup slivered almonds, chopped
1 cup raspberry jam
1 tablespoon lemon juice

1 Finely grind the blanched almonds and 3 tablespoons of the flour.

2 Cream together the butter and sugar until light and fluffy. Stir in the lemon rind and vanilla extract. Add the ground almonds and remaining flour and mix well to form a dough. Gather into a ball, wrap in waxed paper, and chill for 1 hour. Preheat the oven to 325°F. Line two baking sheets with waxed paper.

4 When all the dough has been used, make sure you have equal numbers of rings and circles, then place the dough rings and circles ½ inch apart on the prepared baking sheets.

6 In a saucepan, melt the jam with the lemon juice until it comes to a simmer. Brush the jam over the cookie circles and sandwich together with the rings. Store in an airtight container with sheets of waxed paper between the layers.

3 Divide the dough into four. Roll each piece out on a lightly floured surface to a thickness of ⅛ inch. With a floured 2½-inch pastry cutter, stamp out circles, then stamp out the centers from half the circles.

5 Beat the egg white with the salt until just frothy. Brush only the cookie rings with the egg white, then sprinkle over the slivered almonds. Bake for 12–15 minutes, until very lightly browned. Allow to cool for a few minutes on the sheets before transferring to a wire rack.

Chocolate Marzipan Cookies

These crisp little cookies satisfy a sweet tooth and have a little almond surprise inside.

Makes 36

❦

INGREDIENTS

scant 1 cup unsalted butter
generous 1 cup light brown sugar
1 egg
2½ cups all-purpose flour
4 tablespoons cocoa powder
7 ounces white almond paste
4 ounces white chocolate, chopped

❦

1 Preheat the oven to 375°F. Lightly grease two large baking sheets. Cream the butter with the sugar in a bowl until pale and fluffy. Add the egg and beat well.

2 Sift the flour and cocoa over the mixture. Stir in, first with a wooden spoon, then with clean hands, pressing the mixture together to make a fairly soft dough.

Cook's Tip If the dough is too sticky to roll, chill it for about 30 minutes, then try again.

3 Roll out about half the dough on a lightly floured surface to a thickness of about ¼ inch. Using a 2 inch cookie cutter, cut out rounds, re-rolling the dough as required until you have about 36 rounds.

4 Cut the almond paste into about 36 equal pieces. Roll into balls, flatten slightly and place one on each round of dough. Roll out the remaining dough, cut out more rounds, then place on top of the almond paste. Press the dough edges to seal. Bake for 10–12 minutes until the cookies have risen well. Cool completely. Melt the white chocolate, spoon into a paper piping bag and pipe onto the biscuits.

Ladyfingers

Named after the pale, slim fingers of fairy-tale princesses.

Makes 18

INGREDIENTS

⅔ cup all-purpose flour
pinch of salt
4 eggs, separated
½ cup granulated sugar
½ teaspoon vanilla extract
confectioners' sugar for sprinkling

1 Preheat the oven to 300°F. Grease two baking sheets, then coat lightly with flour, and shake off the excess.

2 Sift the flour and salt together two times.

3 With an electric mixer, beat the egg yolks with half of the sugar until thick enough to leave a ribbon trail when the beaters are lifted.

4 In another bowl, beat the egg whites until stiff. Beat in the remaining sugar until glossy.

5 Sift the flour over the yolks and spoon a large dollop of egg whites over the flour. Carefully fold in with a large metal spoon, adding the vanilla extract. Gently fold in the remaining whites.

6 Spoon the mixture into a pastry bag fitted with a plain nozzle. Pipe 4-inch long lines on the prepared baking sheets about 1 inch apart. Sift over a layer of confectioners' sugar. Turn the sheet upside down to dislodge any excess sugar.

7 Bake for about 20 minutes, until crusty on the outside but soft in the center. Cool slightly on the baking sheets before transferring to a wire rack.

Walnut Cookies

Makes 60

INGREDIENTS

½ cup butter or margarine
¾ cup sugar
1 cup all-purpose flour
2 teaspoons vanilla extract
1 cup walnuts, finely chopped

1 Preheat the oven to 300°F. Grease two baking sheets.

2 With an electric mixer, cream the butter or margarine until soft. Add ¼ cup of the sugar and continue beating until light and fluffy. Stir in the flour, vanilla extract and walnuts. Drop teaspoonfuls of the batter 1–2 inches apart on the prepared baking sheets and flatten slightly. Bake for about 25 minutes.

3 Transfer to a wire rack set over a baking sheet and sprinkle with the remaining sugar.

Variation To make Almond Cookies, use an equal amount of finely chopped unblanched almonds instead of walnuts. Replace half the vanilla with ½ teaspoon almond extract.

Cookies
for Kids

Lemony Peanut Pairs

For those who don't like peanut butter, use buttercream or chocolate-and-nut spread instead.

Makes 8–10

INGREDIENTS

¼ cup light brown sugar
¼ cup soft margarine
1 teaspoon grated lemon rind
¾ cup whole wheat flour
¼ cup chopped crystallized pineapple
2 tablespoons smooth peanut butter
sifted confectioners' sugar for dusting

1 Preheat the oven to 375°F. Grease a baking sheet. Cream the sugar, margarine and lemon rind together. Work in the flour and knead until smooth.

2 Roll out thinly and cut into rounds, then place on the baking sheet. Press on pieces of pineapple and bake for 15–20 minutes. Cool. Sandwich together with peanut butter, dust with confectioners' sugar.

Ginger Cookies

If your children enjoy cooking with you, mixing and rolling the dough, or cutting out different shapes, this is the ideal recipe to let them practice on.

Makes 16

INGREDIENTS

⅔ cup brown sugar
½ cup soft margarine
pinch of salt
few drops of vanilla extract
1¼ cups whole wheat flour
1 tablespoon cocoa, sifted
2 teaspoons ground ginger
a little milk
icing glaze and candied cherries, to decorate

1 Preheat the oven to 375°F. Grease a baking sheet. Cream together the sugar, margarine, salt and vanilla extract until very soft and light.

2 Work in the flour, cocoa and ginger, adding a little milk, if necessary, to bind the mixture. Knead lightly on a floured surface until smooth.

3 Roll out the dough to about ¼ inch thick. Stamp out shapes using floured cookie cutters and place on the prepared baking sheet.

4 Bake the cookies for 10–15 minutes. Allow to cool on the baking sheets until firm, then transfer to a wire rack to cool completely. Decorate with glaze icing and candied cherries.

Fruit and Nut Clusters

This is a fun, no-cook recipe that children will like to make and eat.

Makes 24

INGREDIENTS

8 ounces white chocolate
⅓ cup sunflower seeds
½ cup slivered almonds
⅓ cup sesame seeds
⅓ cup raisins
1 teaspoon ground cinnamon

1 Break the white chocolate into small pieces. Put the chocolate into a heatproof bowl over a saucepan of hot water on low heat. Do not allow the water to touch the base of the bowl, or the chocolate may become too hot.

2 Alternatively, put the chocolate in a microwave-proof container and heat it on Medium for 3 minutes. Stir the melted chocolate until it is smooth and glossy.

3 Mix the remaining ingredients together, pour in the chocolate and stir well.

4 Using a teaspoon, spoon the mixture into paper baking liners and allow to set.

Marshmallow Krispie Cakes

Makes 45

❦

INGREDIENTS

9 ounce bag of toffees
4 tablespoons butter
3 tablespoons milk
1 cup marshmallows
6 cups Rice Krispies

❦

1 Lightly brush an 8 x 13-inch roasting pan with a little oil. Put the toffees, butter and milk in a saucepan and heat gently, stirring until the toffees have melted.

2 Add the marshmallows and cereal, and stir until well mixed and the marshmallows have melted.

3 Spoon into the prepared roasting pan, level the surface and allow to set. Cut into squares, put into paper baking liners and serve.

4 When cool and hard, cut into squares, remove from the pan, and put into paper cases to serve.

Gingerbread Jungle

Snappy cookies in animal shapes, which can be decorated in your own style.

Makes 14

❦

INGREDIENTS

1½ cups self-rising flour
½ teaspoon baking soda
½ teaspoon ground cinnamon
2 teaspoons granulated sugar
¼ cup butter
3 tablespoons light corn syrup
½ cup confectioners' sugar
1–2 teaspoons water

❦

Cook's Tip Any cutters can be used with the same mixture. Obviously, the smaller the cutters, the more cookies you will make.

1 Preheat the oven to 375°F. Lightly oil two baking sheets.

2 Put the flour, baking soda, cinnamon and granulated sugar in a bowl and mix together. Melt the butter and syrup in a saucepan. Pour over the dry ingredients.

3 Mix together well and then use your hands to pull the mixture together to make a dough.

4 Turn onto a lightly floured surface and roll out to about ¼ inch thick.

5 Use floured animal cutters to cut shapes from the dough and arrange on the prepared baking sheets, leaving enough room between them to rise.

6 Press the trimmings back into a ball, roll it out and cut more shapes. Continue until all the dough is used. Bake for 8–12 minutes, until lightly browned.

7 Allow to cool slightly, before transferring to a wire rack with a metal spatula. Sift the confectioners' sugar into a small bowl and add enough water to make a fairly soft icing.

8 Spoon the icing into a pastry bag fitted with a small, plain nozzle and pipe decorations on the cookies.

Chocolate Crackle-Tops

Older children will enjoy making these distinctive cookies.

Makes 38

❧

INGREDIENTS

7 ounces semisweet chocolate, chopped
scant ½ cup unsalted butter
½ cup granulated sugar
3 eggs
1 teaspoon vanilla extract
scant 2 cups all-purpose flour
¼ cup unsweetened cocoa
½ teaspoon baking powder
pinch of salt
1½ cups confectioners' sugar for coating

❧

1 In a medium saucepan over low heat, melt the chocolate and butter together until smooth, stirring frequently.

2 Remove from the heat. Stir in the sugar, and continue stirring for 2–3 minutes, until the sugar dissolves. Add the eggs one at a time, beating well after each addition; stir in the vanilla.

3 Into a bowl, sift together the flour, cocoa, baking powder and salt. Gradually stir into the chocolate mixture in batches, until just blended.

4 Cover the dough and refrigerate for at least 1 hour, until the dough is cold and holds its shape.

5 Preheat the oven to 325°F. Grease two or more large baking sheets. Place the confectioners' sugar in a small, deep bowl. Using a small ice-cream scoop or round teaspoon, scoop cold dough into small balls and, between the palms of your hands, roll into 1½ inch balls.

6 Drop each ball into the confectioners' sugar and roll until heavily coated. Remove with a slotted spoon and tap against the side of the bowl to remove excess sugar. Place on the prepared baking sheets 1½ inches apart.

7 Bake the cookies for 10–15 minutes, until the tops feel slightly firm when touched. Remove the baking sheet to a wire rack for 2–3 minutes. With a metal spatula, remove the cookies to a wire rack to cool completely.

Chocolate Dominoes

A recipe for children to eat rather than make. Ideal for birthday parties.

Makes 16

INGREDIENTS

¾ cup soft margarine
¾ cup granulated sugar
1¼ cups self-rising flour
¼ cup cocoa powder, sifted
3 eggs
For the topping
¾ cup butter
¼ cup cocoa powder
2½ cups confectioners' sugar
a few licorice strips and 4-ounce
package M & M's, for decoration

Variation To make Traffic Light Cakes, omit the cocoa and add an extra 3 tablespoons all-purpose flour. Omit cocoa from the icing and add an extra 4 tablespoons confectioners' sugar and ½ teaspoon vanilla extract. Spread over the cakes and decorate with red, yellow and green candied cherries to look like traffic lights.

1 Preheat the oven to 350°F. Lightly brush a 7 x 11-inch baking pan with a little oil and line the base of the pan with waxed paper.

2 Put all the cake ingredients in a bowl and beat until smooth.

3 Spoon into the prepared cake pan and level the surface with a spatula.

4 Bake for 30 minutes, until the cake springs back when pressed with the fingertips.

5 Cool in the pan for 5 minutes, then loosen the edges with a knife and transfer to a wire rack. Peel off the paper and allow the cake to cool. Turn the cake onto a chopping board and cut into 16 bars.

6 To make the topping, place the butter in a bowl, sift in the cocoa and confectioners' sugar and beat until smooth. Spread the topping evenly over the cakes with a spatula.

7 Add a strip of licorice to each cake, decorate with M & M's for domino dots and arrange the cakes on a serving plate.

Gingerbread Teddy Bears

These endearing teddy bears, dressed in striped pajamas, would make a perfect gift for friends of any age. If you can't get a large cutter, make smaller bears or use a traditional gingerbread-man cutter. You might need some help from an adult with the decorating.

Makes 6

INGREDIENTS

3 ounces white chocolate, chopped
6 ounces ready-to-roll white sugar paste
blue food coloring
1 ounce semisweet or milk chocolate
For the gingerbread
1½ cups all-purpose flour
¼ teaspoon baking soda
pinch of salt
1 teaspoon ground ginger
1 teaspoon ground cinnamon
⅓ cup unsalted butter, chopped
⅓ cup sugar
2 tablespoons maple or corn syrup
1 egg yolk, beaten

1 To make the gingerbread, sift together the flour, baking soda, salt and spices into a large bowl. Rub the butter into the flour until the mixture resembles fine bread crumbs.

2 Stir in the sugar, syrup and egg yolk and mix to a firm dough. Knead lightly. Wrap and chill for 30 minutes.

3 Preheat the oven to 350°F. Grease two large baking sheets. Roll out the gingerbread dough on a floured surface and cut out teddy bears, using a floured 5-inch cookie cutter.

4 Transfer to the prepared baking sheets and bake for 10–15 minutes, until just beginning to color around the edges. Leave on the baking sheets for 3 minutes and then transfer to a wire rack.

5 Melt half of the white chocolate. Put in a paper icing bag and snip off the tip. Make a neat template for the bears' clothes: draw an outline of the cutter onto paper, finishing at the neck, halfway down the arms and around the legs.

6 Thinly roll the sugar paste on a surface dusted with confectioners' sugar. Use the template to cut out the clothes, and secure them to the bears with the melted chocolate.

7 Use the sugar paste trimmings to add ears, eyes and snouts. Dilute the blue coloring with a little water and use it to paint the striped pajamas.

8 Melt the remaining white chocolate and the plain or milk chocolate in separate bowls over saucepans of hot water. Put in separate paper piping bags and snip off the tips. Use the white chocolate to pipe a decorative outline around the pajamas and use the semisweet or milk chocolate to pipe the faces.

Sweet Necklaces

These are too complicated for young children to make but are ideal as novelty Christmas presents. Arrange in a pretty, tissue-lined box or tin for presentation.

Makes 12

❦

INGREDIENTS

*1 quantity Lebkuchen mixture
1 quantity icing glaze
pink food coloring
selection of small candies
6 yards fine pink, blue or white
ribbon*

❦

1 Preheat the oven to 350°F. Grease two large baking sheets. Roll out slightly more than half of the Lebkuchen mixture on a lightly floured surface to a thickness of ¼ inch.

2 Cut out stars using a floured 1-inch star cutter. Transfer to a baking sheet, spacing them evenly. Taking care not to distort the shape of the stars, make a large hole in the center of each, using a metal or wooden skewer.

3 Gather the trimmings together with the remaining dough. Roll the dough under the palms of your hands, to make a thick sausage about 1 inch in diameter. Cut in ½-inch slices. Using the skewer, make a hole in the center of each. Put on the second baking sheet.

4 Bake for about 8 minutes, until slightly risen and just beginning to color. Remove from the oven and, while still warm, re-make the skewer holes because the gingerbread will have spread slightly during baking. Allow to cool on a wire rack.

5 Put half the icing glaze in a paper icing bag and snip off a tip. Use to pipe outlines around the stars. Color the remaining icing with the pink coloring. Spoon into a paper icing bag fitted with a star nozzle.

6 Cut the candies into smaller pieces and use to decorate the cookies. Set aside to harden.

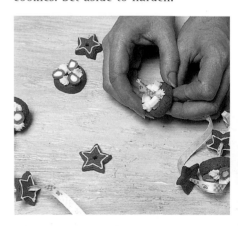

7 Cut the ribbon into 20-inch lengths. Thread a selection of the cookies onto each ribbon.

Chocolate-Tipped Cookies

Get those cold hands wrapped around a steaming hot drink,

and tuck into chocolate-tipped cookies.

Makes 22

❦

INGREDIENTS

½ cup margarine
3 tablespoons confectioners'
    sugar, sifted
1¼ cups all-purpose flour
few drops vanilla extract
3 ounces semisweet chocolate,
    chopped

1 Preheat the oven to 350°F. Lightly grease two baking sheets. Put the margarine and confectioners' sugar in a bowl and cream them together until very soft. Mix in the flour and vanilla extract.

2 Spoon the mixture into a large pastry bag fitted with a large star nozzle and pipe 4–5 inch lines on the prepared baking sheets. Cook for 15–20 minutes, until pale golden brown. Allow to cool slightly before lifting onto a wire rack. Let the cookies cool completely.

3 Put the chocolate in a small heatproof bowl. Stand in a saucepan of hot, but not boiling, water until it melts. Dip both ends of each cookie into the chocolate, put back on the rack and allow to set. Serve with hot chocolate topped with whipped cream.

Cook's Tip Make round cookies if you prefer, and dip half of each cookie in the melted chocolate.

Five-Spice Fingers

Light, crumbly cookies with an unusual Chinese five-spice flavoring.

Makes 28

❦

INGREDIENTS

½ cup margarine
½ cup confectioners' sugar
1 cup all-purpose flour
2 teaspoons Chinese five-spice
powder
grated rind and juice of ½ orange

❦

1 Preheat the oven to 350°F. Lightly grease two baking sheets. Put the margarine and half the confectioners' sugar in a bowl and beat with a wooden spoon, until the mixture is smooth and creamy.

2 Add the flour and five-spice powder and beat again. Spoon the mixture into a large pastry bag fitted with a large star nozzle.

3 Pipe short lines of mixture, about 3 inches long, on the prepared baking sheets. Leave enough room for them to spread.

4 Bake for 15 minutes, until lightly brown. Allow to cool slightly, before transferring to a wire rack with a metal spatula.

5 Sift the remaining confectioners' sugar into a small bowl and stir in the orange rind. Add enough juice to make a thin icing. Brush over the cookies while they are still warm.

Cook's Tip These cookies are delicious served with ice cream or creamy desserts.

Date Crunch

Makes 24

INGREDIENTS

8-ounce package graham crackers
⅓ cup butter
2 tablespoons light corn syrup
½ cup pitted dates, finely chopped
3 ounces golden raisins
5 ounces milk or semisweet
chocolate, chopped

Cook's Tip For an alternative topping, drizzle 3 ounces melted white and 3 ounces melted dark chocolate over.

1 Line a 7-inch square shallow cake pan with foil. Put the crackers in a plastic bag and crush coarsely with a rolling pin.

2 Gently heat the butter and syrup in a small saucepan until the butter has melted.

3 Stir in the crushed crackers, the dates and golden raisins and mix well. Spoon into the prepared pan, press flat with the back of a spoon and chill for 1 hour.

4 Melt the chocolate in a heatproof bowl, over a saucepan of hot water, stirring until smooth. Spoon over the cookie mixture, spreading evenly with a spatula. Chill until set. Lift the foil out of the cake pan and peel away. Cut the crunch into 24 pieces and arrange on a plate.

Peanut Cookies

Packing up a picnic? Got a birthday party coming up?
Make sure some of these nutty cookies are on the menu.

Makes 25

❦

INGREDIENTS

1 cup butter
2 tablespoons smooth peanut butter
1 cup confectioners' sugar
½ cup cornstarch
2 cups all-purpose flour
1 cup unsalted peanuts

❦

1 Put the butter and peanut butter in a bowl and beat together. Add the confectioners' sugar, cornstarch and all-purpose flour and mix together to make a soft dough.

2 Preheat the oven to 350°F. Lightly oil two baking sheets. Roll the mixture into 25 small balls, using your hands, and place on the baking sheets. Leave plenty of room for the cookies to spread.

3 Press the tops of the balls of dough flat, using either the back of a fork or your fingertips.

4 Press a few of the peanuts into each of the cookies. Bake for 15–20 minutes, until lightly browned. Allow to cool for a few minutes before lifting them carefully onto a wire rack with a metal spatula.

Cook's Tip Make monster cookies by rolling bigger balls of dough. Remember to leave plenty of room on the baking sheets for them to spread, though.

Apricot Yogurt Cookies

These soft cookies are very quick to make and are useful for lunch boxes.

Makes 16

INGREDIENTS

1½ cups all-purpose flour
1 teaspoon baking powder
1 teaspoon ground cinnamon
1 cup rolled oats
½ cup light brown sugar, plus some for sprinkling
¾ cup chopped ready-to-eat dried apricots
1 tablespoon slivered hazelnuts or almonds
⅔ cup plain yogurt
3 tablespoons sunflower oil

1 Preheat the oven to 375°F. Lightly oil a large baking sheet.

2 Sift together the flour, baking powder and cinnamon. Stir in the oats, sugar, apricots and nuts.

Cook's Tip These cookies do not keep well, so it is best to eat them within two days, or to freeze them. Pack into polythene bags and freeze for up to four months.

3 Beat together the yogurt and oil, then stir evenly into the flour mixture to make a firm dough. If necessary, add a little more yogurt. Use your hands to roll the mixture into about 16 small balls.

4 Place the balls on the prepared baking sheet and flatten with a fork. Sprinkle with light brown sugar. Bake for 15–20 minutes, until firm and golden brown. Transfer to a wire rack and leave to cool.

Applesauce Cookies

These fruit-flavored cookies are a favorite with children.

Makes 36

INGREDIENTS

1 pound cooking apples, peeled,
cored and chopped
3 tablespoons water
½ cup sugar
½ cup butter or margarine
1 cup all-purpose flour
½ teaspoon baking powder
¼ teaspoon baking soda
pinch of salt
½ teaspoon ground cinnamon
½ cup chopped walnuts

1 Cook the apples with the water in a covered saucepan over low heat until the apple is tender. Cool slightly, then purée in a blender or mash with a fork. Measure out ¾ cup.

2 Preheat the oven to 375°F. Grease a baking sheet. In a medium-sized bowl, cream together the sugar and butter or margarine until well mixed. Beat in the applesauce.

Cook's Tip If the applesauce is too runny, put it in a strainer over a bowl and let it drain for 10 minutes before measuring it out.

3 Sift the flour, baking powder, baking soda, salt and cinnamon into the mixture, and stir to blend. Fold in the chopped walnuts.

4 Drop teaspoonfuls of the dough onto the prepared baking sheet, spacing them about 2 inches apart.

5 Bake the cookies for 8–10 minutes, until they are golden brown. Transfer to a wire rack and allow to cool.

Index